Reading Roundabout

Hearing

Paul Humphrey

Photography by Chris Fairclough

W
FRANKLIN WATTS
LONDON • SYDNEY

First published in 2007 by
Franklin Watts
338 Euston Road
London NW1 3BH

Franklin Watts Australia
Level 17/207 Kent Street
Sydney NSW 2000

ISBN: 978 0 7496 7450 2 (hbk)
ISBN: 978 0 7496 7462 5 (pbk)

Dewey classification number: 612.8'5

A CIP catalogue record for this book is available from the British Library.

Planning and production by Discovery Books Limited
Editor: Rachel Tisdale
Designer: Ian Winton
Photography: Chris Fairclough
Series advisors: Diana Bentley MA and Dee Reid MA,
Fellows of Oxford Brookes University

The author, packager and publisher would like to thank the following
people for their participation in this book: Auriel and Ottilie Austin-Baker,
Bryn Stallard-Pearson, Harriet and Imogen Stanley, Lucas Tisdale,
the students and teachers of Penn Hall School, Wolverhampton.

All photographs by Chris Fairclough except for the following:
P13: Andrei Tchemov/istockphoto.com; pp 14, 18 and 19: Tony Dilger.

Printed in China

Franklin Watts is a division of Hachette Children's Books, an Hachette Livre UK company.

Contents

Five senses

You have five senses. They are seeing, touching, hearing, smelling and tasting.

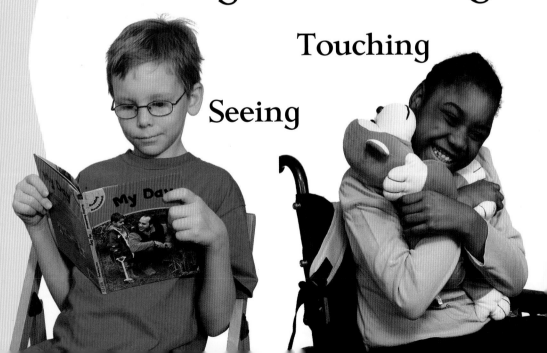

Touching

Seeing

Hearing

Smelling

Tasting

Your ears

You hear with your ears.

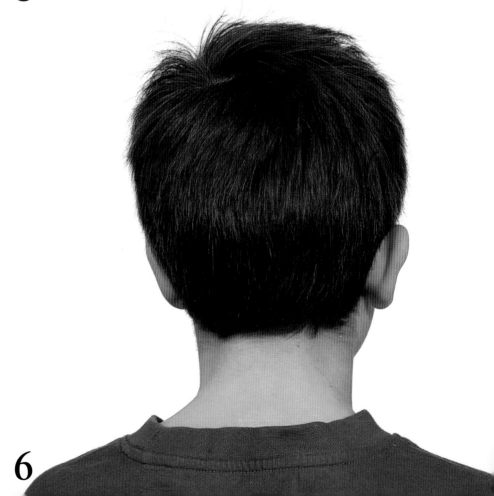

They help you to
tell where sounds
come from.

How we hear

Your ears are shaped
to catch sounds.

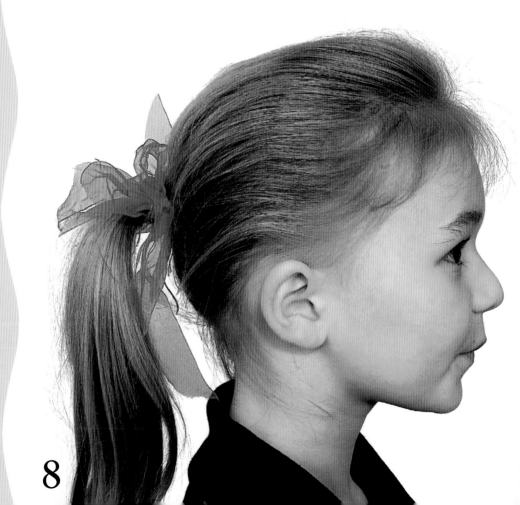

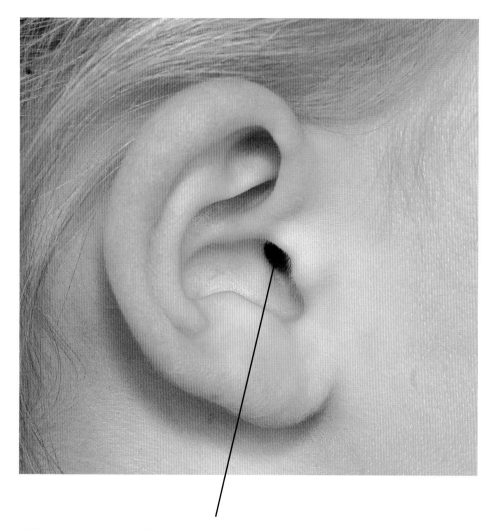

Sounds go into this
hole in your ear.

Listening

With your ears you can listen to music...

...or listen to your friends.

Loud and quiet

You can hear loud sounds.

Whoosh!

You can hear
quiet sounds.

Rustle Rustle

High and low

You can hear high sounds.

Tweet

Tweet

You can hear
low sounds.

Rumble

Rumble

15

What's that sound?

What sound does this make?

Or this?

17

Animal ears

Rabbits have large ears.

They help the rabbit
to hear enemies.

Hearing aids

Some people need a hearing aid to make sounds louder.

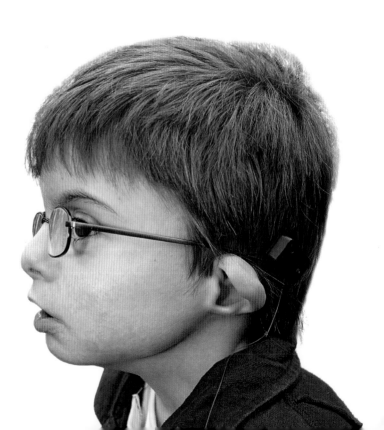

Some deaf people
use sign language
to talk to each other.

Day and night

During the day you hear lots of sounds.

But at night you
need quiet to sleep.

Word bank

Look back for these words and pictures.

Animal ears

Day

Ears

Hearing aid

High sounds

Listen

Loud

Low sounds

Music

Night

Quiet

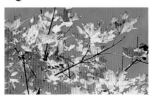

Sign language